Heat Wake

Heat Wake

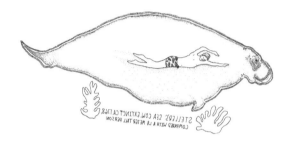

STELLER'S SEA COW, EXTINCT CA. 1768
COMPARED WITH A 1.8 METER TALL PERSON

Jason Zuzga

saturnalia books

Distributed by University Press of New England
Hanover and London

Saturnalia Books
105 Woodside Rd.
Ardmore, PA 19003
info@saturnaliabooks.com

ISBN: 978-0-9962206-2-0
Library of Congress Control Number: 2015945809

Book Design by Saturnalia Books
Printing by McNaughton & Gunn

Cover Art: Jim Drain

Back cover photo: Eddie Cohen

Author Photo: Eddie Cohen

Distributed by:
University Press of New England
1 Court Street
Lebanon, NH 03766
800-421-1561

Many thanks to the editors of the following publications where variations of these poems have appeared: *Canwehaveourballback, Drunken Boat, Elective Affinities, EOAGH, FENCE, Five Finger Review, Forklift Ohio, Gulf Coast, jubilat, Maggy, Nerve, The Paris Review, Provincetown Arts, Tin House, Tupelo Press Quarterly, Volt, White Wall Review, The Yale Review* and the anthology *The Dream Closet.*

The author would like to thank The University of Arizona Creative Writing Program, The Breadloaf Writer's Conference, The Fine Arts Work Center at Provincetown, and the James Merrill House in Stonington, CT for time, residence, and financial support.

Much gratitude for measures of love, encouragement at crucial moments, and invaluable close readings of the poems provided by many, including Agha Shahid Ali, Mark Strand, Kenneth Koch, Franz Wright, Ann Close, Deborah Garrison, Harry Ford, Boyer Rickel, Jane Miller, Charles Bernstein, Jack Hagstrom, Karen Bender, Eric Schellack, Greta Byrum, Kimi Weart, Eric Von Stein, Regan Good, Caroline Crumpacker, Mark Wunderlich, Monica Youn, Michael Tyrell, Brian Blanchfield, John Myers, Stacey Richter, Richard Siken, Jean-Paul Pequeur, Maxe Crandall, Julia Bloch, Jason Mitchell, Cynthia Arrieu-King, Anna Maria Hong, Steven Amsterdam, Elliott Hundley, Matthew Gross, David Gardner, Vincentine Zuzga, Stanley C. Zuzga, Victoria Stracquadanio, John Stracquadanio, Jane Faiola, Andy Emitt, Mimi Romeo, Stanley Zuzga, David Zuzga, Caleb Zuzga, and Zinedine Zuzga.

Thank you to Henry Israeli and everyone at Saturnalia Books.

This book is for Joan Zuzga, who made everything here imaginable and possible.

Table of Contents

3. Electric Clocks Don't Tick

4. What Queens May Come

5. Dead Reckoning

Look not for Whales in the Euxine Sea, or expect great matters where they are not to be found. Seek not for Profundity in Shallowness, or Fertility in a Wilderness. Place not the expectation of great Happiness here below, or think to find Heaven on Earth; wherein we must be content with Embryon-felicities, and fruitions of doubtful Faces. For the Circle of our felicities makes but short Arches. In every clime we are in a periscian state, and with our Light our Shadow and Darkness walk about us.
—Sir Thomas Browne, 1658

And I feel
Quicker than a ray of light
Then gone for
Someone else shall be there...
And I feel
Like I just got home
—Madonna, "Ray of Light"

Delete This Word

Elegy

All rocks are queer. By this I mean
I'm gay. I mean rocks don't reproduce.
They have no future. It's only now.
What I mean is like coal
like uranium like a meteor—

These rocks move from here
to there. With our hand-minds
or a slope. Wind pushes water,
jackhammers make a scenic drive.
Potential energy sneaks up on
this rock and gets kinetic.
The rock rolls down the hill.
The rock stops. It rests
facing this way for the next
forty-three years.

Rocks don't float. Rocks don't sing.
Rocks don't dance. But I love you.

Something happens somewhere
and gravity is turned off. All rocks
float up or not. They tap together.
There is a sound like happy rain.
The rocks fly around. Then gravity's back.

This rock could crush your skull.
This rock could weigh your papers
down in the crazy wind.
This rock is a rock. Inside of
this rock is more rock. For rocks,
it's still night. No light. Even at noon.

All rocks are not hungry. All rocks are
sighing off electrons. All rocks are waiting
for the end of this world, which,
because rocks have no sense of time,
is happening now. There is no wait.
It's over before it begins and
the rock is shining in the heat
of the expanding sun.

All sand is rocks. This rock
if struck with time + lichen + water
would collapse into so much sand.
Potassium. Vanadium. Boron.

The petrified forest,
tree chunks like lost teeth.

The rocks are not tunneling around.
The rocks are not anxious ever after.
The rocks are not tawdry, jealous, or rude.
The rocks are ignoring their edges.
The rocks are full of vibrational music.
The rocks move in your mouth.
You say Antlers. Alcatraz. Abyssynia.
With rocks in your mouth, Atlas.
Argon. Aluminum. Alabaster.
Say these words with rocks in your mouth:
Arginine. Able. Africa. Assortment.
Aspire. Aorta. Australia.
I love you. I do. I love you.

Connected

A long sugar stick—translucence
and transparence—twirled
molecular ribbon—held dark inside
this mouth against this tongue.

Scissor this word from printed fiber.
Let this persuasive stain dissolve
under tongue like a pink snowball
held by mammal hand inside
an aluminum house or
standing in this sunlit creek.

Burn this on a pyre of
scrapped macaques,
research-jangled and car-blown.

Delete "this" with a clap
from air, from the file of words;
scratch this from the sand
with pointed stick.

This through-line will connect
you—to me, whether you be of tar,
of electric, of pheromone
spat through tube.

Ear

You agree to clean my ear.

Pour hydrogen peroxide into a froth
of static, my head, side down, on the sink.

With a washcloth you swab a drop before
it reaches my mouth.

One touch hurricanes you open.

Inside I'm mouthing clouds,
great birds generated at each intersection of skin.

I touch here and you twitch, touch here
and you push my head away.

We lie on the down comforter,
our mouths raw with violet wheat flavors.

I see the surfaces of your eyes moisten.

I will brush your teeth from behind.

Homage

If Rimbaud were here, I would feel shy
because of his green baby eyes and forearms ending
in hands with individual kissable fingers
say not a word until the perfect moment ticks
into place and then he might smirk at me
over his chest his stomach his young french cock uncut
and smooth as the moment is long with life—
I could go for a walk with him one regular
afternoon in the city and say look, things!

City Life

I have trouble with skin, thinking about
how much I love your knowledge, love your mechanics
as your joints do their work. You reach towards the
glass of water. We breathe each other's breath
in elevators, all together now. The elevator
inches up another notch. In a democracy
we can have all the spaghetti we want. We can
choose how to close the mouths of our garbage
bags. Twist ties, or two loose ears of plastic tied into a knot.
Nuns before they take their vows are not nuns.
In the way our eyes are coexistent with our toes,
perhaps our first step is coexistent with our last
breath, but the lazy speed of light doesn't
let our atomic minds figure this. Six men on horseback
exchange jokes and fall in love with each other.
Horses love us for our hands. The horsemen
frolic, spinning in circles, pattycaking with the not-yet-nuns
under the honeysuckle. I consider what it might be if I
could exist in the fifth dimension, to see a whole
life in the way one can turn a cube.

Love Poem

I was angry at myself for being a teenage mermaid, no
tongue, no legs, silly limbed and hesitation as you
sipped beer from a reusable cup.
I was a boy angry at the new hair on your stomach.
I could see the hair when you raised your hand.
I was getting angry at so many things.
I felt disposable. I was in rage.
I hummed on locusts wrapped tight in wax paper.
In love with you, I hauled gash
marks across my skin like mean geese
floating nowhere on a manmade shit pond.
This is going to be what life is like,
the dogwoods chortled, life without plot—
I please request an Edward Abbey burial.
Just hide me under any leaves in the woods.
Please carry my body there.
I won't "read too much into it."
I won't "take it the wrong way."
I please request that my anger be percussive so you can feel it's real.
I want to count my own moments of pleasure at the sight
of you with an aerodynamic adding machine;
when it makes its angry sounds, they shall fasten you to the earth.
They control your steps tap tap toward me.
I am angry at gravity for not flinging you off.
I am angry at math for including you.
And then I am flying and then I am dead
and I am still in love with you.
And then, after everything else is gone—
all my friends back to the bones they were made of,
all my ashes turned to glass by the lightning,

all the atoms of earth wormed to floss by a stray black hole—
it hangs there still at the end of time
like the paddle-tail from the flesh of a freshly pelted beaver.
It droops there dumb, at the end of time:
my being in love with you.

Ten Things in a Jar

This toy is a lady pushing a baby in a perambulator. Wound up,
the lady rushes the baby in circles while the vertical axle spins
out an umbrella over the two, a blue-green beaded blur.

We used this wrench to tighten the beach house pipes for winter.

All the boys wore a bandana like this one year. It was cheap;
the dye ran.

This little hospital marble is small and in fits Victoria Falls.

He didn't tell me this was a cock ring until I pulled it around my wrist.

This is sugarcane from my trip to the tropics, cut sharp and sweet.

Who put this here? It's a napkin corner torn off at dinner.

I ate for the first time without being held from this Pooh bowl.
When there were no more Cheerios or milk there was Pooh in
the air with balloons.

This is a purpled sheet of wax paper used to dry violets.

This is my hand.

All Hands

I am running my skin all
over the place to detect
acrobatic traces, cool
climates up under the trolleys.
Six kinds of nerves streak up
your neck to the planetarium where
my held hand floats and rotates
rendered by holographic projector.

I am holding your hand again, haptically.
I mean the bees in my body are restless again
and want to break out and swarm
you in a vibrating cloud,
return to reveal your whereabouts
with formulaic waggle dances in my brain.

You over there,
eating your sandwich—
all that mouthfeel of kaiser roll, lettuce, and ham—
what are you feeling?
Bring your skin closer so
I can feel how it feels.

Making Butter

(*video transcript*, 2002)

Is this too much?
I think it might be easier to shake if you don't have too much.
We're going to give a little bit to Eric here.
Now we're going to make some butter.
We're going to start shaking it.
Do we have any faster music?
We need faster music, faster music.
This is a workout.
I don't feel anything anymore.
Now, no it's not done yet.
It's whipped cream.
Don't do that.
Wait can we put on faster music.
It's getting heavy.
Oh I got the trick now.
This feels really obscene.
Zero to nothing.
I'm starting to feel it.
Should we test it?
Oh my god
Almost butter.
Oh my god.
Oh my god.
It works.
It's not butter yet.
It's still whipped cream.
Is it butter yet?
No.

This is getting in the way.
There is water leaking out.
It hardened and the liquid is coming out.
Now it's getting into a solid.
I need a plastic bag.
It's like a solid that is flipping up and down.
Oh my god, weird.
Wow.
This is what it actually.
Oh my god.
Oh my god.
We made butter.
Mine is really slippery.
You have to have this milky stuff.
We made butter.

Galaxie Motel

Extinction Narrative

So this is what it feels like
to be crowded into the body
of a Steller's Sea Cow.

It's moving along the tidal rocks
munching on sea lettuce the color
of absinthe. Chartreuse.

You are shifting next to me
trying to get comfortable.
Even though this extinct body is eight meters long,
it's a tight fit for two homosexuals.

The skin is so thick that the icy waters
of the Bering Sea don't register at all.

I feel the warm flesh on my face.
I can feel your arm around
me. I can feel thumps echo from
other Sea Cows, nuzzling ours.

Here come those intrepid explorers.
Let us be pointless.

Little Nemo, Scientist

At the bottom of the sea,
Little Nemo wakes alone,
fallen out of bed
by the edge of his hydrothermal vent.

He clicks on the remote controlled spotlight.
He counts the giant tubeworms bowing forward,
bending back. They are all there.

Back to sleep and in Nemo's dream
there is a cartoon caboose
that seems to breathe.
An evil coelacanth is running
for president and campaigns across the plains.
The once-extinct fish throws wrapped gels to
the screaming crowd. All of this
is more or less in black and white
except for the guy wearing a
pink tank top.
Nemo identifies with him.
Water pours from his mouth.

Nemo wakes from his dream
and finds himself again fallen out of bed
five miles beneath the clapping waves.

He clicks on the remote controlled spotlight.
He counts the giant tubeworms bowing forward,
bending back. They are all there.
These worms have no anuses.

His robot arm slides open to
their giant lipstick length.

The Bats

Animals opening their mouths or mandibles
and talking in the bushes about what they
are thinking. A let me out. A give me that.
A let me put this in you.
That's enough for vocabulary in the zoo.
The crows step about on the lawn
and the gulls careen in the white-walled air.
All I want is to unbutton you, take off your
hat and put my face in it. Here is the goose
from my chest. He takes steps and
climbs up on the dusk.
The best is when I am pressed down
by you, flat and happy, you are breathing
in my ear, no words, just the action of your
body on mine. I am a person now only with a heart
inside going faster and animal and your
hands holding mine back and down
you enter me and my mind shoots out

Under grass, your gait—if I was to bathe
in night rivers of moonshine, dizzy palms
full of fiddles. There are bells for north.
There is walking into town.

West

I store my easterlies in a black box.
I close it to hear sounds at arroyo's edge,
dry as skull, dry as silver.
Listen, stray letters
pinch air. *t t bz k*

The sky veins with electricity.
Perspiration breaks down,
the ground blond and blind, hot deer
hoof the riprap and find you there,
eating soy-milked cereals or popsicles.
You think you can live here.
Sun blinds you.

The readymade earth is fat
because it is spinning. The dark interior bodiness
apples open with a stumble down onto these
broken stones. Erosion a process that
doesn't happen here.
Some forms of silence flourish in the purpose gap.

In a house on the rock live two people.
They die and dry odorless.
In a pocket in the rock
lives a desiccated festival
of toads and beetles waiting for a dull rain.

Moths move among the tall cactuses.
The desert likes the moths because they are silent and dry
and about to die—adult trash in the air.

The desert wears its cactuses like a whale wears lice.
Whales breach to bang itches out of their crevices.
The sounds flick off. Please.
The desert would like to be alone.

You Utah

The whole pile shifts like it's bothered.
Land licked open by rasp cat tongue,

Bunny licked clean of its muscle.
The heave up of furious shouts

Me down in the car, empty
Highway, noon sun and rock blocks.

Galaxie motel, Brigham City.
Key rattle and pork fry.

I taste salt on face. In fingers, it
Hurts. Moisture wants out.

Bones cool bright, the weight a scaffold of dirt
Shivering with things that are not alive.

My clothing. Conversation a bucket. The land
Stands up around me. Shocked rock, I say,

Sit down. My sweat separates into vapor.
White cloths on sticks approach,

Newspaper snapped to wire fences.
Stealth fighters hover, black triangles in blue.

Hands hot on the steering wheel.
Turn now my mouth

To a plastic mouth of water—
Fiji, pacific springs.

Sites

Gravity in sandstone. The little beasties dead
and dropped down to the gooey bottom sinking
and lying one upon another. Angular detritus caverns
of microns, cornfields in Indiana and seals
migrating in the open sea swimming.
A shot of Earth from beyond, in infrared
the heat of bodies, decay and the sloshy core
that stirs the ball and keeps it polished.
New volcanoes spit. I pop the pimple
on your back and the bunched skin turns pink.
The real time tasting and the thermal long sleeve shirt
navy blue on you, the shape of this stage of your body.
One stone pulled from space burns to atoms
in the sky behind you from where I'm looking.
I breathe you in and eat my salad.

Your Age on Other Worlds

Greased surfers on the right,
oil pumping up the left—you drive down the crease
of California as the convexities of boys become
heightened on the waves.

I will guess your age on other worlds.
Stretched into sixteen on all of them. Mine.
When Neptune hurls back around to where it is now
these boys will be decaying
not tucked into their skins not tucked into their wetsuits
not sixteen not alive not riding the waves off California
rubbing itself the way a back shifts.

One night one boy is hurling through time to
the instant he will pass you in the supermarket.
His liverspotted hand a vortex shoves you through
heads of lettuce into the seafoam surfboard
gliding up the crest of time into California.
The pumpers suck sweet sip of time's decay.

The car drives past you down the crease burning rubber.
The oncoming night glides open and closes and pulses.
Observers lightyears away longingly watch wave
lift you. Look back now to where we were before
this got started—star collapsing,
insane and greedy in the dark.

On Being Held

I place a call into the channel
churning atmosphere, poke at you like lightning
making up its mind. We're on hold.
Your ears snap open.

~

The scientists puff muscles to spread shirts out.
A punctured box holds a miffed cat.
Clams rage within the sand.
The octopus roves without a shell.
The octopus snatches the unsuspecting crab,
mashing movement's jointed shell to
fragments within chitin beak.

~

No Olympic sport involves the tongue.

~

What's so great about manipulation, electric tools?
The octopus is not heading toward word's hold.
Osmotic tissue with globule camouflage,
communications dispersed by skin and eyes
among the eight members, nerves an ever-reaching.

~

Autonomous arms explore the scientists's glass mask.
Masks decompress the human eye.
Cornea remains convex in cupped air for better focus.
Any thumb of water pressure
flattens human lens to blurred vision.

~

My friend the scientist, how you occupy your skeleton!
How you sweep your seafloor with driftnets and recount the derby,
guide gradients with a fan of pipettes,
crochet liquid equations, *voilà* the tesseract.
The film of nacre assembles atom by atom
on your sunken matrix in hopes of a pearled screen,
a breakthrough, to hold a moving image flatly in the clear.

~

Imaginary privacy, hedges, bolting futures,
people welcoming relaxed
tentacles onto laminated menus.

~

On the Mediterranean
seafloor, furious competition for
shortage of shelter. Coffee cans,
cannon, amphorae. On a boat, humans lower
traps from stern, ropes baited with shelter:
terra cotta pots. The octopus darts,
gathers in bonelessly sure.

~

The life span of an octopus is too short for words.
They do not tend their young, and
they are not social creatures.
The fisherman hauls up the line,
rips clenched mollusk free,
bites into brain stem, a courtesy.

~

I place a call, and a channel opens.
Your mouth opens. We speak
together in tongues.
What the bodied remember.
What the bodied can do.

Frequency

Sharks have organs in their faces
called Ampullae of Lorenzini
that perceive electricity. No matter
how murky the water, the shark
can hear the signal your brain sends
to your heart to do it again, do it again.
The flounder under the sand.
The lightning miles away.
The politician shaking the hand of
the woman who slips the gun from her purse.

The sea is made of hydrogen, oxygen, and
minerals that compress into skull with spacey eyes
on either side, rocketing toward
the buzz where people are playing.
The lifeguards look high

on their chairs and listen
to the radio making sounds from the air.
The kids are electric, electric and learning
to sail. Do it again, they laugh and climb back
on the boat. The water goes dead.

Argonautica

I unwind some helixes on the beach and slither
beneath the whizzing Frisbees.

I am displaced. I am feeling
new buildings emitting flame or
dome shapes, scalloped towers, jagged
clocks. Cobblestones trip me up and
sometimes a bioluminescent plum throbs by.

I fall into a cloud of bees. They take me apart.
My chips and scraps are sealed in wax and
fed on royal jelly until I puzzle back together
and break the hive open, beclouded
with pollen, pollen on my eyelashes.

The cloud descends before my face.
I see each bee face, each bee eye.
Each eye sees me multiply.

Electric Clocks Don't Tick

Northeast Corridor

At my dad's office picnic, I stepped on a frog. It spoke of itself in the purest way, calling its insides onto the driveway.

The stranger shakes me upside-down. The Swedish fish that was choking me pops from my mouth to the elevator floor. Red blob like a kiss mark.

Eric plays the comb with wax paper from the ham sandwich his mother made for the long car ride. Tillman Ravine, sawed into northern New Jersey. There were orange salamanders everywhere. He placed one, cold, in my hand.

Aunt Dottie liked how the mint could overtake the lawn, wrap itself all over the woodpile. She made sun tea, mint leaves suspended in jars stacked all over the patio. Toweled dry, we grabbed glasses from the tray.

After a few highballs, Vincentine marries Grandpop, teaches me how to polka at the wedding. Stepping quick between these faces, we move like carbonation, like vodka.

Simma's grandmother is dead. We eat pickled beans with thin metal chopsticks. The marinated anchovies nest in Tupperware, eyes glazed with soy sauce and sugar. Touch the huge warm pot of rice beside the refrigerator. Feel the hum of the refrigerator motor.

Dad helped dig Kennedy's grave. When we are in Arlington Cemetery he has me stand where he stood when they called him over.

The blue flame beneath the ravioli at the graduation party.

Mom picks wax beans in the backyard, puts them in a paper bag. She lines the elephants on the shelf.

The iron bog boom-town of Ong's Hat is missing. We cruise the sand roads of the Pine Barrens in Paula's Crown Victoria. Ong threw his hat up once and it never came down. The pines swallow in one thick motion. The town is supposed to be here, right here.

Mounds of honeysuckle behind the basketball court.

Bite the base of the flower and pull the stamen through.

He is from Chile. I see the map of the streak of country tacked up on the wall in his dorm room. After an hour of maneuvers, he turns off the light and we fumble for each other in the dark, slipping on stripped-off sweatshirts, is that you is that you is that

One does not expect two pairs of llamas on Block Island.

Sam's mom comes in to talk about a painting for Art in the Schools. Her impeccable fingers hold the frame as she talks about color, the billion dots that are this picture. Sam can turn his eyelids inside out. Gross! We inch closer. *Sam, make them like that again.*

The ice bulges huge and blue. I listened to her stomach for the heartbeat. I remember how we took the magnet letters from her mother's refrigerator and spelled "veramapatilogatizakibenys," then hid a pitcher of gravy behind a box of cereal until the gravy grew fur. The bus churns past the steel barriers. The clumps of ice bulge from the cliffs and none of it falls to the road.

On the cliffs by Bar Harbor, he can see his uncle die again. His uncle lies gasping in the Econolodge, slow creeping shudder, mouth a taut ring. My brother and I hide in the clothes racks. Fountains surround the food court, shining out the noise.

In the iron bog, the rust clouds shift through the water in huge blooms that streak the cedars.

Aunt Florence peers through the chained door, unfastens the lock, won't budge; *white flight, white flight*, she sighs. Gulls swoop over Camden. In the Polish church, I fool with the spring hook that holds the mass book. *Snap bang. Stop that! Peace be with you.* After she died, *and also with you*, Dad finds hundreds stuffed under the mattress.

Mom shakes the water from the washed lettuce. Her sons pull up the slate slabs of the pool path, looking for bugs. She hollers *dinner* through the screen door, *come in and wash your hands.*

Chocolate Milk Puzzle

There are four kids sitting at the cafeteria table drinking chocolate milk. There is a man lying under the table. The air, hot and close, compresses as the sound of the fire drill rockets outwards three-dimensionally from the metal knob and its internal little freaking hammer.

There are four kids sitting at the cafeteria table drinking chocolate milk.
        The air, hot and close, compresses as the sound of the fire drill rockets outwards three-dimensionally from the metal knob and its internal freaking hammer.

There are four kids sitting
        under the table. The air, hot and close, compresses as the sound of the fire rockets outwards three-dimensionally.

There are four kids
        under the   air, hot   the sound of the drill   the metal knob and hammer.

There are four kids sitting
        three-dimensionally.

There are four sitting at the   table drinking.   There is a man lying under the table. The air, hot and close, compresses.

There are four   rockets.

        There is a man
        hot and close.

Outwards   little   hammer.

There   There is a man.

Reagan

Second grade: he's shot.
In the armpit. Ouch that stings.
I enlist the second grade in a simulation of
Escape from Witch Mountain. I am picked
last for kickball. I kick the air hard.

All night the green lights in the trees are
spies; home is not a building; it is us.
My dad meets Reagan at a dinner and shakes his hand.

I stay home sick from school.
My friend Jennifer comes over
and tells me how at lunchtime
one girl had swung a whole loop
around the swing set, got tangled up in
the chains and broke both her arms.
That was a lie, a good one.

Encyclopedia Brown Saves the Day

The kidnapper was Carl, who owned Alfred.
He found the seat was cool.
The clue was the coffee pot.
For the boat, floating on the tide, would have risen too!
Mules simply cannot have offspring of their own.
He could not have jumped through a shade and closed window!
Electric clocks don't tick.
The real bird watcher walks west so
the sun's full light comes from behind him
and falls on the birds.

Three Lucies

One is fifty years old trapped in the body
of a thumb-size two-dimensional girl.
One is shawled in the scent of boiling
tomatoes, garlic and talcum powder.
One is winding in waves drunk on vitamin
juice forever giving birth in her secret red hair.

Lucy Van Pelt pulls the football away.
Lucy Ricardo smokes six packs a day.
Lucy Pappa sits in her wheelchair on her grey stucco porch.
You must kiss her loose cheek.

If you say "lucy,"
these three are who I see,
Lucy pushing the wheelchair—
Lucy, Indian-style, on the soft lap of Lucy.

~

Lucy doesn't get it, she couldn't care less
about namesakes, animation, or wheelchairs.
Refracted through time, she walks within diamond.
She smokes a single cigarette upon the rift.
She spins the bottle. She starts the game.

Brother Poem

Off the coast of Hawaii,
manta rays swarm a cone of incandescent light:
grand pianos undulating into sight.

What I want to do is write an elegy for the rabbit Kip,
named after a long distance runner.
My brother David lived with the rabbit,
just the two of them.

There was the dog, wet and alone, and there is my brother following
its lank white arc from doorway to doorway in Philadelphia, waiting
for trust that comes after hours and hours of slow-following,
respecting distance, and here is the lost dog with bleeding sores and
an infected eye lifted up into the air into human my brother's arms
Sammy dog the now named dog.

John Hill Esq. conducts an experiment in 1670.
All is atoms, he presupposes.
He grinds a leaf into pulp with mortar and pestle
and stirs the pulp into a metal cup of water from
his English well. He believes all is atoms and attractions,
and the film of ice
on the surface of the water
formed in the country night
proves him right,
provides pressure enough to allow
the pestled atoms to bind back together.
Hill, in the chill of morning peeps into the metal cup,
and through the clear ice film
he sees the leaf hovering in the water, reconstituted,

until his eager jostle cracks the hold of frozen skin,
and the leaf disperses back to its constituent atoms.
No longer held together by the pressure of a skin,
the ghosting leaf in water disappears.

There was a rabbit enclosed in one life in one body.
Grunting, it circled any standing leg and humped by leap,
little rabbit penis straining like an attaboy noodle.

I have a brother who may be doing something now
in Philadelphia, maybe sleeping or doing his homework.
I know for sure that a few weeks ago he lifted his pet rabbit into a box,
took the box to the veterinarian and said
it's time before he could say anything else.
The tip of the needle pierced the skin of the rabbit,
and David my brother placed his hand on the rabbit's back and kept it there.

My brother and I stand by as our dad Stanley tries to breathe
but he can't any longer, so the ambulance comes to our house.
They place him onto a wheelchair, but there isn't time to navigate
the lawn, and he is very fragile. So they lift the wheelchair up
and carry him above and across the front yard like C3PO mistaken
for an Ewok god, the gold droid's chair raised up through
Luke's use of the Force, spun slowly in mid-air as
a demonstration of his power.

anemones ingesting

arctic hare with massive feet
the boat slices the water in two

if not Dad, the water is staying here with us for the time being

the air is staying here with us for the time being

rabbit, we

Oh what magnificent pianos we may find to hammer on—
My brother and I find some right
here when we turn the corner,
a discarded pile of pianos half collapsed and twisted
together, just asking to be
jumped on and clobbered,
banged on and whacked
as hard as one can hit.
My brother and I smash
on them, making

broken music
in New London

by the Sound.

My Parents' Bathroom

One thing I could do was shake talcum powder into a Dixie cup of water. It created an odd film; I could stick my finger into the water and my finger wouldn't get wet. I'd stick all sorts of things into the water, Q-tips and a bit of eye shadow off from one of the nestled bricks in a compact. Eventually the bottom of the Dixie cup would become so soggy that the paper would tear. Under hot water, the cup pulp reduced to nothing. All the paper dissolved down the drain except for one thing, the clear plastic disk that had guarded the base. I put it on the back of my hand. I couldn't see it, but I could feel it there until it dried.

I could watch the pool from the bathroom window. The serrated air vent poured air-conditioned air around my ankles. Our backdoor neighbor, Mrs. James, would come in the late afternoon, after we were done swimming and had gone inside to watch *Star Blazers* and *General Hospital*. I would take a shower in my parents' shower and then watch Mrs. James do the backstroke through the blinds. She was an adult and alone in the pool, with arms that loped up and through the air, down into the water, like the power of water and trees. There was a confidence in her large blue bathing suit that I couldn't fathom. It made my feet feel small.

Hamper and scale. Hair dryer and curling iron. The plug-in makeup mirror with variable lights that could make your face look like it was evening, like it was inside, like it was spring.

I could put a container of soap on the drain so that the water began to fill the shower stall. I would take the Paul Mitchell shampoo and drizzle it all over myself so I smelled like a coconut afternoon. I would sit down on the yellow tile and let the shower shower me, drawing my hair down in waving lines over my face, and try and breathe, the watery breaths, the taste of pipes. All the steam that I was cubed in thinking of the tropics, linen skirts through the fanning palm fronds, the opalescent whale song replenishing everyone's skin. I would lean forward and rest my forehead on the tiles, the plumbing of the whole house working all around.

Poem for My Mother

This is a new house for my mother to live in.
Here is a lazy room with walls of birds.
The sofa in it contours perfectly to read on, velveteen
worn soft. The birds are white doves.
The birds are flamingos of coral snow,
wings rustling, capable grandchildren grasp feathers.
The window looks onto a garden of rosemary breezes.
Any rain's spray braids itself, mazing down the masonry wall.
There is an observatory on the top floor. A spiral staircase
takes her there, where she may walk and look upon the sea,
the railings painted black, high above kind neighbors. The glass dome
of the central tower opens to the pour of in-brightening sky.
Here's the moon who returns, spangles
the sturdy willow in ringlets of silver. And the stars—
makers-of-jewels. Each night they come to her,
again alive. The ivies cool the halls and warm them
according to need, a room of stretching meditation,
a room for ballet. The bedroom is woven of living eucalyptus
that announces her life to the dawn. Her name
scrolls in fragrant rose-purple blossoms,
aromas of coffee and chrysanthemum teas.
And there are monkeys. Outside. They smile
and hand her apricots washed in the stream.
They want to give her houses.
They want her to pat them on the head and sing them
certain lullabies that fertilize the grove.
Here's a door to close against their need.

Therapeutic Aesthetics

That blue swirl with the twinkling lights
is my anxiety about money.
The red slash with hairs
is my anxiety about my health.
The orange crescent is my anxiety
about my family members—what
are they doing now. Are they Okay.
I'll reduce them to dots.
My dad's stomach surgery was reduced
to one bitter flavor, glass of snifter bulb
holds within the swirling herbal fumes.
The dots swell in my brain
as I recline by the window—my
brother walks down the street
to his lab, my mom pours
hot water. I look at the orange
pulse of brushwork.
I can see the steam
as the people run hollering
along the cold sand.
The eye of the beached pilot
whale reduces to one pixel.
I massage its struggled breath
to a stretch of slivered line.
I walk along the silver line to get some coffee.
I feel the black bile rise in my throat.
I slide the bile into its proper place:
one of four corresponding humours.
One hundred years from now,
I will not exist, I remind myself.

I place that thought through the mouth
of a tall glass vase, a pool of filtered
water. I watch it bloom and wilt.
I watch my face distorted in the bulb.

What Queens May Come

The Riddle

The sphinx tore at my brain with her riddles.
She transformed me into a creature
that was front-half lion, back-half deer.
I took a bite of my own flank and digested myself.
I was nutrition enough to allow the wound to heal.
With a twist of the sphinx's claws,
I swapped halves, lion tail swishing, mouth of herbivorous teeth.
The back half of me wanted to rush
into the front half of me.
I wanted to roar but only nibbled at the grass and tipped
back onto my muscular lion haunches, haplessly kangaroo.
My lion half demanded more protein, the muscles
aching and starved.
My deer half was all brain and considered this.
I bit a few birch leaves, masticated, ears aflutter,
sniffing myself and feeling alarmed.
The wind came thrusting through trees
considered me in the way.
I breathed in the wind. I stopped
a mouse with my hind claw.
The sphinx turned the mouse into grain, stalks erupting
through its face and back, I nibbled on them,
considering the sphinx as she folded me into her wings.

Invisible Friend

Let us begin with a variable x.
Say x = pebble. Glitched

stem becomes a will itself,
negotiates with bend.

Bend will signature
the self, a calligrapher's brush against cliff

makes a name: greet
rise-left catch-in-throat.

When you sound said name, thank
the obstructions: ask for an axe, a cracked quill,

ask for the wrong tool to make a mark.
In a felt kiss, the obstructions

sound wrong. Tag. Study.

Your square root entangled
on a lit match of impossible intaglio:

image of cliff becomes wrinkled
disclaimer. Open, kiss—

Counting

A glisten of sixes coming at me from the night sky
twirling—these numbers are bingo—too close—I twin
and fall down the stairs. The you twin watches the I twin
tumble laugh bruise and combustion. Those incredible breakfasts
with their softnesses that meet your fork.
This is another breakfast in New Jersey
with the family. Tricks with salt and eggs.
Now college is a wheelie—I see a school bus fall
through the ice, *The Sweet Hereafter* dubbed in French. Montreal
comes all over me, summer running down
the night street with a fountain full of detergent
suds bubbling into the air on my left
and a boy I just met tight in my right hand.
We are speaking in French and Italian and English.
We run to the river—there you strip off my
clothes, we start kissing, plus more,
until entirely covered with happy juices
and cut grass. I go to the same place
a week later, and there is a dog
that I photograph twice. One of me is in Canada,
the other one of me is in Rhode Island,
trying acid the one and only time,
ricocheting bop bop bop around campus
to a mattress on his floor by a sultry window.
The window frame shimmies and shakes—she gets down
from the wall, turns into rectangular gospel singer.
"Do anything to me that you want you can do anything,"
he says in my ear. I don't know what I want, but I roll with him
under some sheets, and it's like there is a squadron of men,
one kind and epic team of smiles, wrestling our arms
around each other, kissing each other's legs, bursting up
from the ice with, in one hand, the school bus full of kids
cheering, in the other, a fork
with a number of us spiked loose on the tines.

The Leonids

The Leonids—hot streakies spitting
through Leo, sad lion with his question mark star mane.
I stand in my shorts, up from lawnchair and my chile relleno,
walk over to where I was sitting with a guy
drinking Dos Equis, a six-pack, last week.
I was trying to find his mind, hair on his hind legs.

You and I looked up to see the cool flashes
of long-lost comet tailings spit flare
above such scraggly tress that last year
we were headed through to beach to see.
Lobes of blankets, my head on your breathing chest.
In the fire, potatoes wrapped in aluminum foil.

The same trace of ice ball glitz leaves streaks,
coming and going oval to Pluto.
You pin up new sights in Los Angeles, self-sufficiency
your piled wall of pinned styrofoam boulders.

I am here, looking up,
mealy-mouthed, lighthouse-mouthed.
My emotions desiccated like a pinpoint
tardigrade (common name: Water Bear).
They can desiccate, hibernate a hundred years aloft.
They can zing with the gusts—live
particle dust—until from some
cloud's one cool drop of rain
draws a straight ray down to moss which says
wake up Water Bear resume your life
fill out your six fat legs barrel your torso
suck yourself up on these my moist threads.

Barrel cactus says wake up to me,
perfect height to bite my knee
hard with its fishhooks. Fuck, I shout, and jump
in this sand bowl, this sector of solar system.

My shout sends the prickly pears into ecstasy, their
paddles fall off, thump down to floor.
The cat eats bees and waits at the door.
North of the Catalina mountains,
Biosphere Two goes to ruins, glass domes
hold collapsed aspirational ecozones.
The neighbor undergraduate with
his SUV winks at me, and his eyes sparkle.

Oh Eastern Seaboard, I was in bed with you,
lightly scratching your long arms.
My friend Caroline calls,
we miss you, she says
and I say I miss me too.

Hoover Dam

Hoover Dam understands
if you have to go to the bathroom.

If you tempt me with your smile,
I will encase you in gelatin.

I love you porkchop, you say to your porkchop.

I love you porkchop, you say to your doom.

You cast seed onto the field
and shape a soft maze.

The penguins' speed is such that they shoot up
ten feet or more then plop down onto the ice.

Fifty million soup labels will buy them a basketball.

The ocean with three fish left.

We all sleep alone, says Cher.

The last box of low-salt Triscuits. Half full.

Liquid Courage

I open a volume of fluid to find myself
swirled in a pile of morning sheets, into the eye
of a cute peer facing me from an old photo tacked
to a wall, this wall or that player piano. A volume of fluid
has limit if not shape, a titratable number of drops.
I think that I may have exceeded the number of allowable
falls-in-love. My volume is fluid, my limits fixed.
I buy another laptop. I buy a new phone.
I find myself at this door again, a goat's eyelid secure in my pocket.
Further elapsing. You're not a kid anymore, they say.
You're not a gorilla anymore, they say.
I find my way again across the moors.
I sit on a sofa, and I think I am not the sofa, but
the screen blocks the view to my feet.
The shale yields another billion cubes of natural gas.
A bright sloth orphanage glints
from the screen within the screen,
the CBS evening news again unspools
the surprise eruption of Mt. St. Helens.
A nuclear reaction lights a city, crests as
a deer attacking a man gets a billion hits.
A retirement account burps along quietly, insane as the night.
During my lifetime another volcano explodes or does not.
Yellowstone blasts up a perfect circle of light.
These are not my memories.
This is not my screen.
My volume is fluid.
My memory is set to repeat.

Heat Wake

Oh ye not-yet elephants of Mars,
marching cross the red rock plain.
Ye not-yet ants and not-yet rats,
love there as you might the sands.
New guns are already there.
We have hollowed out a time,
a way to press ourselves into a not-yet present.
They will have that much to count upon.
It will be wrapped and pinned.
Unromantic over time.

"Falling in love instantaneously is convenient
and romantic, and it occurs in literature
more than in life." In the future,
am I not alive? Is Ava Gardner not
by the sea, singing alone upon the balcony?
Not now, but Now.
Not yet, but Smaller.
Then. Shall we be there to hear the ping.
Generator, generator. Take me, take my hand.

Will there be love paid hours, a contessa purse
with standard megan click.
What fashion will words be made of
then and of what willfulness.
We have hollowed out a time,
a funnel to press ourselves into a pocket.
Will we be there already
when we get there by rocket.
Everything in storage in the cave
has been stirring, metal with the engine brains.

I send a shout through to you,
my beloved elephants unextincted.
And to you my sweetly speeded giant sloth and
knuckled dolphins with your tripod claws,
towered ants of hexagons and turrets,
mossy forests waving encrusted forgots.

Mutant whistle, the sensate drips.
Impossible to impede the bloom.

I saw the pinked waves swoop up and
drop beneath the pirate's plank—
as we stood together, toe to toe,
gathered: prick of sword.
That sensation! At our backs,
feel it pinch a point in time.

And if I this hour fall in love with power's open hand.
And if I this day fall in love with language.
I can take some oomph upon my back and lift a sad sack
woven from a word, wring words to make a ladder.
I can monitor the turbines if you need me to.
I can grease a palm with shadow. I can
sprinkle kitten round your tear ducts when you're down.
Generator, generator. Take me, take my hand.

Say "I am not in love."
Say "The Life that puckers forth a me."
Say "sea shimmer cat jellies."
Say "palm tree." Say "pine tree."
Say "Walruses shove the air, aloft, gone thinner by the arm."

In the future will there be such songs?
A tusk to find the groove.

Once say here upon a time—Ava Gardner,
your loose fitting clothes become you.
I become your light motes. Cigarette smoke
tailing up through the cone of projected light.
I see you and I sail a skin upon a beam,
the Idea of Ava Gardner by the sea,
translated into binary code.

A digital breath, scattering words blown
like limes upon the sand.
Wrong to say alas the end.
Wrong to say alas the ants.
Wrong to say alas oh bumbling gentlemen,
lift your drone ends high and secure the hive,
yourselves now to be forgotten, it's nothing
you did wrong, it's nothing superficial.
Say wrong with your mind's mouth:
then what Queens may come.

It's okay. We've already been dead for hours.
A herd of buffalo rained down upon me
and then and there I died.
It was mine, it was yours, it was a skin.
Wrong to say alas.
Generator, take my hand.

The mermaid's hiss. A gentle kiss
and the headache from the g's.
The glimmer getting bigger.
Upon the wave a room of wood
with enamel handles and mask of lace
placed upon her still'ed face.

The cyborg elephants lift her aloft,
the batteries lashed within their giant backs
spit blue flame that licks methane
through their jointed scales.
The belly burbles in the grave.
The corncobs swatted down
by giant sloths upon the moon.

It shall be so cool there.
It shall be so cold there
inside the future.

Dead Reckoning

Lullaby

Just rest now—the cascade of days will form
a lion on your shoulder. Watcher, companion
as the final solar storms begin.
There is a house inside your medulla oblongata.
There, retract now and reduce.
There are mice in the barn; there are lions riding up
on Ferris wheel, waiting for their turn to exit.
New Jersey spills out lights and trees.
The pines weep a resin as the iron creeks' rangy orange
rust clouds loom in grooves toward
Egg Harbor. Love is a kind of yeast, a fungus
that breathes things into you. A cataract of love
in New Jersey may be between one voter and one driver.
Under the numbers, the dollars, the mint pounded coins.
Just rest now. This is all there is. The atom at
the end of your eyelash, your shoulder a
savannah, a rhymed expanse of skin detected
by satellites. Imagine something they can't see.
Cerebrum. Lion. Iron oxidized. Philadelphia.

Erotic Partial Burial

Take a bulb planter and core down your reach.
Feel the soil crumble and its pressure, kiss partner's lungs,
let your lungs be how your partner breathes
on a cold night. Try this in the dark. Keep
your arm locked in dirt for a long as you can as
dirt's hug should feel spooned, close as pudding.
Squirrel a pit in the peat and lie down
with the dead's dispersions in half-lives and singlet.
Scene of the graver enclosures, pressures in
crushings, and lift minds to corn starch flecked
gravy clawed molecules misting root
mouths' tornado and precipitate sprinkle of ash, fish
bones and lye, atoms spinning betwixt, proud kid
goat on shed. Now sun out, click the nimble
wild wall, the skin that works the inside trick,
tricked out and contained with throbbing
releases, desire's mingling and these worms'
soft mouthed pokes. Your might and your face under pond.
There rub your clay foot in root gag and swallow,
going gulp kiss, you liver a burrow
of hot piss and quiver. Sore the core lava, fissures
upthreading flash footholds and bright mantling hands.
Now with a thumb, do brush the soil from these intricate weaves
of your partner's brow, he looks lovely, locks in chuckled oak.
You look magnificent, make-believe eyes blue brown and pupil.
See that iris a lightning, see may storms across grained eyes.
Fused fingers of opaque glass become prisms
of lovers burying arms, paired feet, two by two, two by two,
down into the tickle of the dark cool, under sand.

Lucy in the Vines

Suddenly again I've swallowed my words, accidentally with the stuffing,
Some may choke on this, some may fail to attach to the uterine wall.
I shaved this morning from my face. I don't know a neck I don't like. I
think it was when you were holding me from behind, I mean there was
that one time, that one time you turned your face to me in sleep I
threaded your lashes. The integral of this kiss measured in bundles of
dwindle times night. I'll need another this-kiss soon then. I'll need a
comic mammal to remind me of the improbability of pants. Each warm
fear snowballs. They are easy to box if you can muffle fear scent in
shipment. For startle you can toss them to bang, just in case no one
believes in platypus again, nor the forgery fairie, Sweet Marie-of-the-
Mesa, nor the astronaut left behind in the excitement of launch, nor the
people transiting taverns by dirt under loft light of link-boys. If I believe
in myself, I will believe in them, well certainly that can't be enough to
ensure my lawful standing. Unsatisfactory. The mere fact of standing.
In the meanwhile, a squall of snow whorls the valley. I look up from the
bed at my fingertip and in the whorls a labyrinth of wheat field,
snowmoon and rabbit-by-proxy spins forth to skip steps. I can't say I saw
any of these icons at the crossroads, only a sign swinging in the wind, a
symbol clanging like a cow bell, a big church swinging by a skyhook,
pendulum & pendulum. An unnoticed cubic inch in the pure space
announcing what herald holler hither or hollow, what holiday jauntily
lurching through a half-ass business lunch followed by dinner in the
ruins. What will kill the appetite is exactly how and why the great ape
falls from the top of the building, no matter the question of how much
you might care. I'm ready to accept lenses to correct my double vision
and settle for only one moon in the sky. I must mourn that twin or I
must take off my glasses or try further triangulation, I may gain position
by dead reckoning, backing up to count the seconds till the thrown rope
tugs taught by pull and count my knots, know my onslaughting slap of

absence-right-here. With each successful landing, another deplanes, another forsaken fantasy island in reruns. Have you achieved matter? Learned of it and us by grid and silhouette? Have you visited each trepanned terrazzo room? All shall these ruins testify by thine own fragrant bouquet that we have carried you, randomly generated child, now for such a time in a sling of skin. We have done so without even knowing. You at great risk to our own mental health were launched from the aerie's tin roof into the atmosphere and light. We have fashioned your imaginary feathers upon our backs, just as we have trekked you through ideas of elephant and games of operation, that you passed from rovers to rovers defined by our provisional equations, the slope of your algorithmic descent paired to the decibel of error's buzz, the curl of later's argosy. And where have your hands been, making forbidden marks, hugging yourself justly tight to just another tree ring, another mere swipe of axe, another trusted house gone vacant as we speak inside of each wave, behind frosted walls of remaining exhalation. Claim this part, plant your flagless pole here beside the Geiger meter. Oh Gepetto long-in-the-tooth, cobbler asleep amid tactical elves, conscripted pirate apprentice, quothing raven, sweetest Lucy-in-the-Vines…come step forward into time. You, there. Yes you there boygirl, napping senseless in the catapult. Shall you become real and trapped in temporary life? What shall you bring forth if we—the ones who shall be doubtlessly lost behind in time—what if we who shall be forgotten do choose to let you live. If we choose to let you live alone as you have thus beer far and caged and done or if we choose to replace you elsewhere with a version of ourselves. If we may choose to put you with another. What would you like? What would you choose for us to choose to let you do.

Dewey Beach

Scuba Rule: Remember to continuously exhale slowly while ascending. As the water pressure decreases and returns to that of one atmosphere at sea level, the air within your lungs will be expanding exponentially. If the air within the lungs isn't cleared continuously, you may explode.

Slate-blue angora flatware: the sea today,
buckling hands of wave foam over cold feet; coast
weighting heels cup deeper into sand.
From where the dolphins slip
up to air we are neither believable or
doubtful, unthought, unseen. We see them as
we are holding hands like what else are we supposed to do

standing here in Delaware in a light rain. Beyond the horizon,
sleeping sickness thuds in tse-tse needle nicks.
Ebola spreads with care. Why am I thinking
of sickness, looking east, the breeze is whipping
your scarf like a jam jar thrown in a jam jar toss, like a purse
blossom, like a gown enthused atop a steeple.
The light and your curly hair pins you down as a festive location,
like a world's or county fair with many booths: snack trailers with whipped
flavors, unexpected fancy chickens, mirrored spheres, fired wavy glass.

At the high tide line, the flecked oyster shell bits make wavy lines,
as do blown black reeds, dunes of wind-heaped sand.
You in the distance, next to me—approaching long.
I buckle fear of you or of an us behind my eyes.
I tie it to my gut, I grab a gull to chest and push it through my ribs,
the ovoid of thicket feathers takes over.
Free heart and lungs fly up as kites in the dim storm.
The fins in the distance toggle.

I ogle you as you walk a bit ahead of me on sand, turning back ensmiled you
walk and I don't know, no I do, I have learned the length of you,
a year ago. A year before that. To you, I mean, what happened
as you listened to (this much I know) your dying father shout you down
as you drove him along the lake, as you sunk below the pitching sun
with your sister, both of you wide-eyed and locked together
by this, not your father but your mother dying first.
The Floridian clocks ticked on with
possible experimental procedures that,
one might say, did no lick of good.

You were nine. I was fourteen when my dad died,
cancer esophageal, then liver. My mom left behind,
her breast and skin cancers now, for the time being, cured.
It is likely that we have both inherited the undertow of cancer.
One kind made of unmoored child and the other
ignorant of age, first a single cell gone mad with
self-involvement, fruity exponential, then
malignancy, as one cell slips loose, aloof from mass,
flouncing in between the tissues, undetected,
feeling blindly for a bloodfed roost to mutter only of itself.

Now we are adults with adult brains inside our skin-swaddled skulls,
no two the same—but our loveable faces try on relationship like a pair of pants.
Getting four legs in slowly, with extraordinary awkwardness,
sibling-esque shoves—but the rough awkwardness feels smooth,
easy as two dolphins shooting through the water's sleeve.
Still I can't fathom, you, me, matter fathoms us,
this person or that one, that cell or that human or this landscape
in which we, to someone else, become an H when we hold hands and stand.

That letter or we're simply faggots. Two sticks in the sand,
two figures active with the lonely lovely rainy day, terror of others.

The beach is empty, of course empty is idiom, nothing is empty.
I am sensing the scooping of life, my life so acute as this tunnel to yours opens
through this or that illness and this or that parent, this
kissing in the Sandcastle Motel.
Fear ebbs where fear was and should be. Anxiety pops away
like a flossed seed, like the wrong word lassoed with a flick of wrist in
twizzler red ink. You are here, edited in, bare feet on sand beside me as we

become one activity of walking and looking,
and later, one thing composed of two unlike selves in the heated motel pool.
In that liquid we pretend to race, exhale to sink down
to concrete floor to mime a quick tea with extended pinkies.
You are executing the underwater handstand like an underwater
handstand pool pro, not to be looked at, I mean, not for my benefit,
but just as what one must do. I am waiting underwater for you,
you in your new polka-dot bathing suit and waterproof skin. I am diving,

walking slowly down the steps into the chill, adjusting step-by-step.
I am terrified of drowning but I have waited down here
at the bottom of the pool, for years, sitting
in my self at the bottom of the sea until you arrived as a ping,
then your pair of slate-blue eyes opened.
The rain perseveres. We perverse in the water.

My dive weights throw down at the sight of your legs,
self throws down as I unhand myself over to buoyancy.
Worry snaps, it rips right away, raw like teeth cracked from jaw.
The bubbles pull me up against my single will to where
you breathe the air inside this cedar-paneled room.

The Sea Cow

Notes

Love Poem

Edward Abbey left behind after his death instructions for the disposal of his body: "No embalming, for Godsake. No coffin. Just an old sleeping bag... I want my body to help fertilize the growth of a cactus or cliff rose or sagebrush or tree."

Extinction Narrative

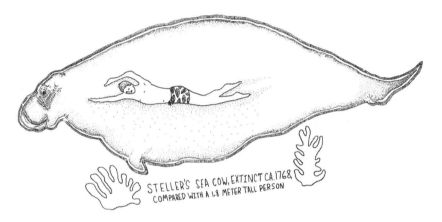

STELLER'S SEA COW, EXTINCT CA. 1768, COMPARED WITH A 1.8 METER TALL PERSON

Drawing by Tracy Stewart

Little Nemo, Scientist

Winsor McCay's comic strip *Little Nemo In Slumberland* ran weekly in the *New York Herald* and *New York American* from October 15, 1905 to December 26, 1926. In each strip's last panel Nemo awakens from his antic dreamings—usually with a bellyache caused by too much dessert.

Brother Poem

Hill had no proof to offer of what he saw except his word.